Contents

SOCCER HOMEWORK

Skill Drills for 1 to 3 Players

Charlie Inverso

Library of Congress
Cataloging - in - Publication Data

by Charlie Inverso
    Soccer Homework
        Skill Drills for 1-3 Players

ISBN No. 1-59164-034-2
Lib. of Congress Catalog No. 2002094142
© 2002

Editing
Bryan R. Beaver

Front Cover Photo by
Robyn McNeil

Printed by
DATA REPRODUCTIONS
Auburn, Michigan

Reedswain Publishing
612 Pughtown Road
Spring City, PA 19475
800.331.5191
www.reedswain.com
info@reedswain.com

INTRODUCTION

There has never been a better time to be a soccer player than today! The opportunities that exist for young girls and boys are almost endless. Young players have the opportunity to travel, play in front of large crowds in great venues, and even receive college scholarships. The possibility of playing professionally in the United States or abroad is greater than ever before. Possible fortune and fame await those who are ready to work for it. There is only one problem. While every player wants to reap the benefits of a dream career, not every player is willing to do what it takes to get there.

 Training for soccer on your own could make all the difference. The exercises in this manual could help you achieve your dreams.

This manual was created for several reasons. Most young players think that playing organized soccer is the only way to improve and training without a coach to improve their skills has never crossed their mind. Many players simply don't know how or what to do in order to improve their skill. Many players simply don't feel it is necessary to work on their skill development. Players must practice on their own. Those who put the time in to work on their game usually show **TREMENDOUS IMPROVEMENT**.

If you strive to play at a higher level, consider the following as initial steps toward reaching your goal:
- Play for a good coach in a good environment.
- Get plenty of challenging games against quality competition.
- Participate in good pick-up or street-soccer games whenever possible.

- Never turn down an opportunity to play.
- Practice on your own using the exercises in this manual.

This manual explains practice exercises and training ideas from some of the top players and coaches in the country. It shows you how to practice on your own or with two or three other players. Consistently using the exercises in this manual will improve your skills. By practicing with the ball in a realistic, pressured environment you should see significant and possibly even dramatic improvements in your game! This manual emphasizes developing a better touch and better control, being able to play the ball faster, improving shooting skills, heading, defending, passing accuracy, the ability to hit long balls and crosses and other valuable soccer skills.

A Note to Parents and Coaches:

Many parents are concerned about their son or daughter's development in soccer. Often they will do almost anything to ensure that their kids will have the best environment to succeed. Most if not all of that development will come in the form of organized games and practices. Organized games and practices are very good for player development. However, they are usually not enough to get a young player to the next level. In some cases the organized soccer environment is actually stunting the player's development. To really get to a higher level of play the young player must practice for hours with a soccer ball, perfecting the various skills necessary to become a good player. This manual can help your son or daughter become a better player. It can also be beneficial to coaches to give them ideas to help design productive training sessions.

How to Use This Manual:

Most of the exercises in this book can be done on a practice field, near a wall or a kickboard or in any open area.

Many of the exercises can be practiced alone. Others are set up for two or more players. PB and PC refer to Players B and C. You take the role of Player A.

Use your creativity when training to best utilize the practice facility and the number of people present. For example, exercises listed under the section "Exercises for Two Players" can also be practiced by 3 or more players. This is true for all sections of this book. Improvise or alter the exercises to suit your needs and make the exercises as challenging as possible.

Required Equipment

The exercises in this manual can be practiced almost anywhere. No elaborate equipment is needed. Some of the exercises require eight to ten balls, but others require only one. Ask your coach or teammates if you can borrow a few soccer balls. Using several balls will save you from chasing during the exercises and will make the practice more efficient and more fun.

You may also need:

- A wall, fence or kickboard, which is anything sturdy enough to rebound   a shot or a pass
- A small kickboard or table
- A full-sized goal for older players, small goals for young players
- Cones or markers

Setting Goals:

Any player who wishes to achieve his dreams of becoming a great player must set goals for himself. A player cannot expect to succeed without a plan. Here are some suggestions which will help you achieve your goals:

- Find a field or facility where you can practice.
- Find a group of players who will show up consistently to practice with.
- Plan your weekly schedule around your practice schedule.

- Everyone is busy. If you don't organize your weekly and daily schedule you won't find the time to improve your game.
- Play pick up games of soccer as often as possible. These games will give you the confidence to try certain things that you might not feel comfortable with in an organized game.
- Always try to find the best competition. Playing against better players and older players will improve your speed of play and understanding of soccer.

Setting goals is an important way to gauge your progress and a vital component of your journey toward being the best you can be on the soccer field.

Here are some tips for setting goals:
- Make your goals realistic.
- Believe in yourself.
- Don't make excuses when you experience a setback. Learn from the mistake and move on.
- Understand that achieving your goal will require many hours of hard work and some difficult experiences along the way.
- Don't let anyone sway you from believing that you can accomplish what you want to accomplish.
- Find a player who is already doing what you want to do and find out what he did to achieve his goals.
- Be patient. It takes time to improve. Don't expect greatness to happen overnight.
- Enjoy the journey and make the hard work fun.
- Remember that all the work that you put in will be worth it in the end.

EXERCISES FOR ONE PLAYER

Even when there is no practice partner available, you can still challenge yourself to improve your skills by practicing juggling and dribbling, and using a wall, portable goal, or kickboard as a substitute partner.

EXERCISE A1:
Juggling for all players
Goal: To develop a feel for the ball and to improve balance and coordination.

Tips for Doing This Exercise:
- Younger players should practice lifting the ball by rolling it back with the soles of the feet and clipping the bottom of the ball with the instep.
- Practice juggling using both feet, your thighs and your head.
- Juggle the ball from your foot to your thigh to your head and repeat.   **ADVANCED SKILL**
- Juggle the ball up in the air several times, let it bounce once, and then start juggling again.
- Juggle the ball, speed dribble 10-20 yards and then juggle again.
- Juggle while walking
- Try using different types of touches, such as using the inside or the outside of your foot.

- Juggle the ball, kick it high in the air, control it and then continue to juggle. **ADVANCED SKILL**
- Stand in front of a goal, juggle the ball and volley the ball on net. Next try juggling the ball, letting it bounce once and hit a half-volley on net.
- Juggle with a smaller ball, preferably a #4 or mini ball, because it is more challenging, requires more concentration, and breaks the routine of regular juggling.
- Combine juggling while practicing other skills such as passing, shooting and dribbling. An example of this would be to pass the ball continuously (one and two touch) against a wall for 1 minute. Stop and juggle for 1 minute and then continue passing against the wall.

Exercise A2: Using a wall/ kickboard
Goal: To improve footwork, passing accuracy, and speed of play.

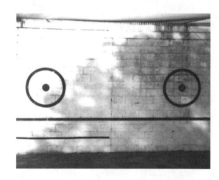

Pick a spot on the wall such as a specific brick or some other marking. Try to hit that same spot as many times as possible from a comfortable distance. Use all types of passes and put time constraints on yourself so that you must play the passes increasingly faster.
To enhance this exercise, try the following:
- Play one or two touch.
- Play two touch by controlling with one foot and passing with the other.
- Play 3-4 quick touches on the ball before passing it.
- Play INSIDE/OUTSIDE. Control the ball with the inside of your right foot, make a quick touch with the outside of your right foot and play the third touch back with either foot.

- Cut the ball behind the planted foot before passing it.
- Use different types of first touches on the ball before passing it. (See Exercise B2).
- Use different types of body feints before your first touch on the ball. (See Exercise B2)

Exercise A3: Targets on a wall/kickboard
Goal: To develop passing accuracy

Place several targets on the wall at various heights, using tape.
- Try to hit each spot from a dead-ball shot.
- Try to hit the same targets while passing, shooting, or chipping off the dribble.

You may also use the wall or kickboard to do many of the shooting exercises listed in Section B 18-39.

Exercise A4: Controlling Air Balls off a wall/kickboard
Goal: To develop the ability to control high balls

Kick or throw the ball high off the wall and control it with your chest, thigh or foot. If you have an additional wall or kick board you can pass or shoot the ball quickly after controlling and turning with the ball.

Exercise A5: Passing off the wall/kickboard
Goal: To develop the ability to play accurate passes and control bouncing balls.

With tape, mark a spot on the wall one to two feet off the ground. Practice passing the ball over the tape as well as under the tape. Playing a pass over the tape will force you to take the next touch controlling a bouncing ball. You don't have to alternate between passing over and under the tape if it is not the correct pass to make.
Practice mixing up one and two touches and alternating

between the right and left foot. After controlling the ball try using some of the touches listed in section B2.

Exercise A6: Kickboards and walls
Goal: To develop the ability to control, turn and play an accurate pass.

Add a kickboard (for example, a wall, a sturdy table placed on its side). This set up will give you two surfaces that will rebound your passes or shots. Practice the following:
- Pass the ball off the kickboard, turn and shoot at the wall. Utilize some of the shooting exercises in Section B. You now can do all of the shooting exercises in Section B that require another player to play a pass to you.
- Pass the ball off the kickboard, turn and pass or chip the ball at targets on the wall.

DRIBBLING EXERCISES

Dribbling is a skill that can be practiced on your own and is one of the most exciting skills you can develop and perfect. However, it takes a lot of hard work and the proper environment. The ideal conditions for developing dribbling skills exist in 1 vs. 1 confrontations. Test your dribbling ability by working against a defender.
Many of the world's greatest dribblers developed their skill in environments where pick-up soccer or street soccer is prevalent. In some parts of the world, including the United States, there is little or no informal street soccer.
Organized league youth soccer, which often discourages individual flair and dribbling development, is more common in the U.S. than in other countries. With restrictions placed on many youth players within a team environment, what is the best way for you to improve your dribbling skills?
All soccer players need to develop basic feints and fakes with the ball. This enables them to hold onto the ball under pressure and be more effective on the field.

Learning to dribble is a trial-and-error process that must be perfected through repetitive exercises that are enjoyable. Set up game-like conditions in informal small-sided games to feel comfortable taking on an opponent and trying new moves with the ball.

Exercise A7: Slalom Dribbling
Goal: To develop the ability to change direction and speed while dribbling.

Set out cones in a staggered pattern. Practice dribbling for speed-in and out of the cones. Practice cutting the ball sharply around the cones using your instep, the outside of your foot and the inside of your foot.
Here are some dribbling moves to practice (all of the moves are described from a right-footed player's perspective).

MOVES TO RELIEVE PRESSURE

- **Spin turn**-with the ball on the outside of your right foot, and while shielding the ball from an opponent, step over the ball with the right foot and cut it with the outside of the left foot in the opposite direction.
- **Chop the ball** across the body with the instep to avoid pressure.
- **Pull the ball back** with the sole of your foot to avoid pressure.
- With your back to the goal and while shielding the ball from an opponent, touch the ball several times with the outside of the foot while spinning the defender around in a circle. If done correctly, a player can go from playing with his or her back to the goal to facing the goal.
- Shield the ball then use a **burst of speed** to go past the defender.
- Use a **fake kick** before the ball comes to you to freeze the approaching defender.
- **Cut the ball behind** the planted leg if the opponent over

plays you to one side.
- **Step turn**-dribble in one direction, step on the ball with the sole of the foot and go in the opposite direction.
- **Fake kick**. Fake a kick and pull the ball back behind the planted leg.

MOVES TO GET PAST A DEFENDER

The "Matthews" Dribble

Ball on right foot.

Player transfers weight with a step on the left foot, getting the opponent to lean the wrong way.

Player puts ball on the outside of right foot and accelerates away.

- **Fake kick**. Freeze the defender by faking a shot then accelerate.
- **Step over**. Step over the ball by rolling your foot over top of the ball (without touching it) and accelerate by the defender.
- **Matthews Dribble (see above)**. Dribble the ball on the inside of the right foot and move inside from the sideline toward the middle of the field. Plant hard on the left foot and accelerate by pushing the ball hard in the opposite direction using the outside of the right foot.
- **Step over the ball**, inside to outside, with the right foot and accelerate by pushing the ball with the outside of the left foot.
- **Fake a heel flick** and accelerate.
- **Body swerve**, using the hips and shoulders to get the defender going in the opposite direction. The player must sell the fake to one side and accelerate to the opposite side.

Players rarely accomplish good dribbling with preconceived moves. Most good dribblers use their instincts and are able to read and react to the defender's stance, feet, and body position.

Good dribblers are usually able to cut the ball with the inside and the outside of the foot. They also make good use of body feints and swerves with the arms and hips. Most good dribbling makes use of change of direction and change of speed.

HOW TO IMPROVE COORDINATION, AGILITY, AND SHARPNESS WITH THE BALL

Many players have a problem with being too stiff and not agile enough when possessing the ball. Listed below are several moves that you can practice by yourself which should help you develop coordination and sharpness while in possession of the ball. After you feel comfortable doing the moves, try combining two of these moves together to develop into one fluid movement:
- Chop the ball with your instep.
- Cut the ball hard with the outside of the foot.
- Pull the ball back with the sole of the foot.
- While dribbling, step on the ball (kill it) with the sole of the foot, then take it away with the outside of the other foot.
- Step over top of the ball (without touching it) with one foot, then take it away with the outside of the same foot.
- Touch it back and forth quickly using the inside of the right and left foot.

You should combine two of these moves to create a practice rhythm, which will help improve your agility, coordination, and sharpness with the ball.
For example:
- Dribble with the outside of the right foot several steps, step on the ball (kill it) with the sole of the foot, shift your weight, take it over with the outside of the left foot.

- Touch it quickly several times with the inside of the right and left foot, then pull it back with the sole of the foot.
- Roll the right foot over the top of the ball, then cut it away with the outside of the same foot.
- Pull the ball back with the sole of the foot, then cut it away with the outside of the foot.

Exercise A8: Shooting
Goal: To develop the ability to put shots on goal

Listed below are shooting exercises that can be done by yourself utilizing a wall, kickboard or a full size goal:
- Dribble laterally (your body should be half turned toward goal) across the top of the penalty area (or closer to goal), turn and shoot on goal.
- Bounce the ball out of your hand or flick the ball up in the air, run onto it and half-volley it on goal.
- Place targets on a wall or a full size goal. Try hitting the targets off of a dribble. Try hitting curling shots with the inside of the foot as well as shots with the outside of the foot.
- Dribble at speed for 5-10 yards and hit a shot on target.
- Slalom dribble in and out of cones and hit a shot when you pass the last cone. See Section A7
- Kick or toss the ball up, control it with the chest, foot, or thigh and shoot.
- With your back to goal or kickboard, toss the ball over your shoulder, turn and shoot.

 SEE SECTION B "EXERCISES B18-39 for additional shooting exercises. You can utilize an additional kickboard for any exercise in Section B 18-36 that requires a pass from a teammate.

Exercise A9: Free kick Practice
Goal: To develop the ability to hit free kicks.

A free kick specialist can change the course of a game with one strike of the ball. The ability to swerve a ball swiftly and accurately can be developed individually.

To practice this skill, make a wall by placing sticks, flags or brooms inside the holes of cones. Anchor the cones so they will not fall over. The set of cones will represent a defensive wall during a free kick. Most successful free kick specialists aim for just slightly over the wall, around the wall, or at the heads of the players in the wall, hoping that the players duck or deflect the ball into a dangerous scoring area. There is no way to "cook book" this skill. It must be developed with lots of practice. Most free kick specialists try to hit "banana kicks" by coming around the outside of the ball and slicing off a shot using the inner section of the instep. Some players look for an opening in the wall to drive the ball through. Everyone has a different style of scoring on free kicks. This is why it takes endless hours of practice to perfect this skill.

So, keep practicing! Just like hitting a great volley, there are few skills in soccer more exciting and more rewarding than scoring on a free kick.

EXERCISES FOR TWO PLAYERS

Exercise B1: Developing touch
Goal: Developing passing skills, ball control, and a better first touch.

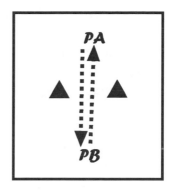

Stand about 6-8 yards away from PB (4-6 yards for younger players) with two cones placed in the middle between you. The cones should be about 1-1.5 yards apart. The higher your skill level, the closer the cones should be.
You and PB should two-touch pass the ball through the cones as many times as possible in a one-minute time frame. Concentrate on playing the ball as fast as possible.

Repeat the exercise with the following conditions:
- Play one touch
- Play two-touch so that you must control the ball with your right foot and play the return pass with your left foot. Then use the same procedure starting with your left foot.
- Use three or four quick touches. This exercise will improve your footwork and touch and help you develop faster feet.
- Play two-touch controlling the ball with the inside of your right foot and playing the second touch with the outside of your right foot. Then try it using your left foot. This is called front foot passing.

INSIDE/OUTSIDE. A more **ADVANCED** exercise is to control with the inside of your right foot, make a quick touch with the outside of your right foot and play the third touch back with either foot. (This exercise, which should be done with both feet, can also be done starting with the outside of the foot for the first touch.) This exercise requires quick movements from the feet and hips.

Try using combinations of all of the passes listed above.

Tips for doing these exercises:
- Be creative with your touches; don't always rely on the basic, inside-of-the-foot pass.
- Get the ball back to your partner as quickly as possible. Practice passing the ball with the outside of your foot. Some coaches call this front foot passing because you use the foot that is in front of you (or closest to your partner).
- Keep your passes clean and low by hitting the middle or top part of the ball. You have done your job properly only if the pass you send to a teammate can be controlled.
- Challenge yourself to play the ball as quickly as your body and mind allow. Don't play too fast for your abilities. Make this an exercise or game in which you are always trying to better the number of passes you can complete within a set time limit or improve on the passes sent to your partner.

Exercise B2: Faking and Feinting
Goal: Adding different touches and body feints to passing skills.

Using the same organization as in the previous exercise, concentrate on adding different fakes, feints, and touches. Use a body fake before your first touch on the ball; for example, swerve or lunge to the opposite side of the first touch or fake a kick before the first touch. Use different types of first touches on the ball before passing it back to PB. The following are examples:
- Cut the ball behind your planted leg.

- Pull the ball back with the sole of your foot.
- Drag the ball sharply across your body with the outside of your foot.
- Chop the ball across your body using your instep.
- Touch the bottom of the ball with your toe or the outside of your foot to put a little lift on the ball. This is a skill you can use in a game to lift the ball over a defender's foot to avoid a tackle.
- On the first touch, roll the sole of your foot over the top of the ball.
- Combine any two of the touches listed above. Also, see Section A, **How to Improve Coordination, Sharpness, and Agility with the Ball**.

Tips for doing this exercise:
- Imagine a defender is covering you or approaching you.
- Create little fakes and feints that will freeze or deceive defenders for just a moment, allowing you a little more time on the ball.

Types of passes to practice:
- Inside of foot.
- Outside of foot.
- Instep chop or reverse pass. This pass can be used to play the ball across your body with the instep and is effective when facing one direction and chopping the ball in the opposite direction.

Concentrate on making clean touches and balancing and adjusting your feet before passing. Anticipate where you want to play the ball and how you should adjust your body to receive and pass as efficiently as possible.

Exercise B3: Call a number
Goal: Developing quicker feet and minds.

Stand facing PB about 6-8 yards apart. Play a pass on the ground and immediately call out a number [1 through 4]. PB must play the ball back using the number of touches that you called out. It is essential that you call out the number immediately after passing the ball.
Variation: Use the same organization as in the exercise above, but this time toss the ball underhand to PB's chest, feet, or thigh and immediately call out a number [1 - 4].

Tips for doing this exercise:
- Try moving after passing to give PB a different target each time.
- Be creative with your touches and passes. Don't be afraid to try something new and different.
- Get the ball down to the ground quickly

Exercise B4: Turning
Goal: Developing the ability to turn with the ball while playing with your back to goal (This exercise requires 8-10 balls.)

Face PB standing 10-12 yards apart (See diagram). PB has several targets [flags or cones] placed behind him or her, anywhere from 12-20 yards away from PB. Send a pass to PB, who turns and plays an accurate pass to one of the flags/cones. (Instead of using cones, PB could try to pass to targets on a wall or kickboard.)

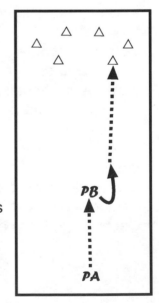

Tips for doing this exercise:
- Never underestimate how important it is to be able to turn with the ball, especially if you play a position that requires you to play with your back to goal.
- You should be able to complete this exercise in two touches. You should turn using one touch and use the second touch to pass.
- Practice hitting the targets with the outside of the foot.
- Under pressure during a game players need to sense an opponent behind them so they don't turn into a tackle. Taking little glances over your shoulder will help develop this ability. This skill can also be improved by using the arms to feel for opponents in tight spaces and by the player who passes and yells "Man on" or "Turn". Players who have mastered the skill of turning in a close space have played against experienced opponents and develop a feel for an opponent's pressure and know whether and where to turn.

TYPES OF TURNS TO PRACTICE
- Inside of foot.
- Outside of foot.
- Cut behind the planted leg.
- Chopped away with instep.
- Drag the ball sharply across your body with the outside of the foot.
- Put a little lift by hitting the bottom of the ball when in a tight space.

Additional tips for doing this exercise:
- Don't always wait for the pass to reach you. Come to meet the pass.
- With your back to goal, if the pass is ready to be played always be alert and ready to come back and show for the ball. *If possible, come back to the ball at an angle. This allows you to receive the ball in a position where you are half-turned to the goal.*

Additional Exercises

Exercise B5: Turning and dribbling
Goal: To develop the ability to turn with the ball and dribble.

Play the ball to PB, who turns, dribbles a few steps, turns, and then plays the ball back to you.

Exercise B6: Advanced turning exercise
Goal: To develop the ability to turn with the ball and switch the play with an accurate pass

Part I
Set up short and long targets as in Exercise B4. The short targets can be 12-20 yards away and the long targets can be 20-30 yards away. Play a ball to PB, who must turn and hit a short or long target with a pass or chip. This turn is different from the turn in Exercise B4. In B4 the player turns with the ball while playing with his back to goal. In this exercise the player, PB, tries to switch the ball from side to side. PB should have his body halfway turned to the side he is switching the ball to. This is an extremely valuable skill (switching the point of attack) for all players to practice. (See diagram)

Part II
Set up a competition with PB using the exercise above (Part I) for one-minute intervals. Keep score, counting who can hit more targets during that time period. You can enhance the competition by awarding additional points for opposite foot passes and outside of the foot passes. For an additional challenge, try to control passes played to your chest or thigh. The goal in this exercise is for both players to turn and play passes quickly, with as few touches as possible. **ADVANCED**

Exercise B7:
Soccer Squash
Goal: To improve agility
and develop the ability
to play and control pass-
es and bouncing balls
quickly.

Use a wall or kickboard for this game. Tape a line on the wall about 2-3 feet from the ground. The boundary lines on the ground should be about 6 yards wide and 8-10 yards long.

Play two-touch and play the ball above the line. Your opponent is allowed two touches and must play the ball above the line. The ball is only allowed to bounce twice on the ground before it is returned. When the ball cannot be returned, rolls over the endline or bounces more than twice, the player making the pass scores a point. Also, try playing the game so that the ball is only allowed to bounce once.

Play the game using the same set up except this time the players must play the ball below the net.

Change the number of touches allowed to alter the difficulty of the exercise.

Exercise B8: Soccer Tennis
Goal: To control the ball using one
or two touches.

Create a small tennis-like court on the ground (6 yards wide and 8 yards long) with a centerline. Keep the ball in play by playing it to your opponent's half using either one or two touches. Agree upon the height at

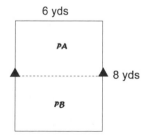

which the ball should pass over the mid-court line. Find an object to use as a reference point for height.

Exercise B9: Controlling air balls
Goal: To improve foot speed and the ability to control balls out of the air.

Face PB, standing 4-6 yards apart. PB tosses the ball underhand to your thigh or chest. You must return the pass using two touches with your instep or the side of your foot.

Tips for doing this exercise:
- Try playing the ball back with the outside of your foot.
- PB should move to give you varying passing targets.
- Do the exercise while jogging backwards/forward as a pair, or side to side.
- Get the ball down to the ground quickly

As a variation, stand 15-20 yards apart. PB tosses or punts the ball into the air for you to control. You should play the ball back to PB using two (one to control and one to pass) touches.

Exercise B10: Pair Juggling
Goal: To develop a better touch on the ball, improve balance and coordination.

Practice juggling with PB. Count the number of touches before the ball hits the ground.

Tips for doing this exercise:
Here are some challenging conditions to place on this exercise:
- Limit the number of consecutive touches allowed by a single player to five.

- Specify the kind of touch a player must use each time he or she gets the ball. For example, the player must juggle it at least once with the outside of the foot before sending it back.
- The return pass must be above your partner's head.

Exercise B11: Volleying
Goal: To make accurate passes and shots from volleys.

Stand about 4-6 yards away from PB. PB tosses the ball to you; you volley it back to PB with the inside of your foot. Once you master this skill, have PB toss balls for you to volley with your instep.

Tips for doing this exercise:
- Point your toe down
- Lock your ankle
- Make contact with your knee over the ball

Exercise B12: Side Volleys
Goal: To improve the ability to volley balls coming at you from the side.

Use the same procedure as in the above exercise, except this time PB does a side volley.

Tips for doing this exercise:
- Sit on the ground facing your partner and practice volley-ing. (Lead up drill)
From a standing Position:
- Drop your opposite shoulder down in an effort to get your leg parallel to the ground and fully extended
- Extend your leg out straight upon contact.

- Don't swing the leg too hard and miss making contact. The ball is moving fast enough. Just make solid contact with the ball.

If you are having difficulty with volleying, practice hitting the ball off of a tee, such as a cone. Work from this stage to where you eventually can hit the ball from a partner's toss. Continue working on this skill until you can volley from crosses.

Exercise B13: Developing a quick first step.
Goal: To develop a quicker first step and to get to balls that are not played directly to the feet.

PB tosses the ball underhanded to you; you volley the ball back to PB with the inside of your foot or your instep. The tosses from PB must be a step or two away from you so that you develop a quick first step.

Repeat this exercise with PB passing on the ground to you. Use one- and two-touch passing to get the ball back to PB.

Exercise B14: Smash Ball
Goal: To develop a softer touch on the ball

Stand facing PB about 8-12 yards apart. Play smash ball with PB. Play passes that are harder than normal so that the receiving player must develop a softer touch to settle and control the pass.

Exercise B15: Chipping
Goal: To develop the ability to hit chips, crosses and long accurate passes

Stand facing PB about 20-30 yards apart (younger players should stand 12-20 yards apart). Try to chip the ball back and forth onto each other's feet. Younger players can practice chipping to their partner's hands.

Tips for doing this exercise:
- Lean back slightly as you strike the ball, but do not be too stiff or mechanical.
- Hit the bottom of the ball and follow through.
- Do not approach the ball straight on.
- Put your planted leg slightly behind the ball.
- Younger players under the age of 10 can take a little air out of the ball to make it easier to lift.
- Practice hitting a moving ball once you master chipping a dead ball.
- Touch the ball forward before chipping it, or chip it off after controlling a pass coming in to you.
- Have your partner make a short run into a target area. This is a particularly good exercise, especially when you make the pass as you are dribbling. Keep your head up while dribbling so you can see your teammates.
- Practice chipping and curving the ball with both sides of your foot. **ADVANCED**
- Dribble forward or sideways a few steps then try to hit a target with a chip.**ADVANCED**
- Take a pass from your partner, turn with the ball, and chip it to a target. **ADVANCED**

Exercise B16: Controlling and Chipping (Advanced)
Goal: To develop the ability to control and play chipping balls quickly.

Play two-touch with PB using chips and curving balls. This forces you to control the ball cleaner on your first touch. This exercise is very difficult. If you do not control the ball cleanly on the first touch, you should take another touch to get the ball under control before chipping it.

Variation:
See how many chips or curving balls you can play to each other in one minute while trying to play two-touch. This forces you to get a clean first touch and to play the second pass quickly.

Exercise B17: Short stride chips
Goal: To chip or cross the ball without using a long step or approach to the ball.

Line up 8-10 soccer balls in a row, about 6 inches apart.

PB should be positioned 20-30 yards away, depending on your leg strength. Try to chip the balls, in succession, to PB without backing away and using a long stride onto the ball. Find the best place for the plant-foot to get height, but don't lose control. This is a trial-and-error exercise that can be very valuable in developing your ability to play a long pass while under pressure.

Also try playing a pass on the ground to PB, who purposely controls the ball close to his body, creating a situation where he must use a chip without a long stride onto the ball.

SHOOTING
*Before beginning the section on shooting be familiar with:
TYPES OF SHOTS THAT SHOULD BE PRACTICED
1.Balls that you run onto
2.Balls that run across your body
3.Balls that are rolling back to you
4.Bouncing balls
5.Shooting off the dribble
6.Volleys and half volleys
7.Shooting with the outside of the foot
8.Turning with a pass and shooting

*Note: What should you do for shooting exercises when there is no goalkeeper?
Set up cones or markers in the goal or attached to the net that must be hit in order to score points.*

Exercise B18: Shooting Exercises
Goal: To develop better shooting technique

Part I
Alternating with PB, hit dead ball shots into an open net, at a kickboard, or off a wall from 18 to 20 yards away. If shooting into an open net, in order to determine the proper shooting distance, you should be able to hit the back of the net with the shot.

Part II
You can also set up an exercise where you and PB are shooting at each other, using cones or portable goals. On defense, you and PB defend your goals as goalkeepers. This exercise can be a lot of fun, especially for younger players. Players need to take special precautions regarding goalkeeper safety. Precautions that should be taken:
- Knowing how to dive properly
- Knowing how to catch a shot

Use the following shooting exercises in the above format:

Exercise B19: Practice shooting a moving ball. You and PB should each touch the ball once (hit a moving ball) before shooting (2 touches total).
Exercise B20: Shooting with the outside of the foot.
Exercise B21: Chop the ball with the instep back to the opposite foot before shooting.
Exercise B22: Lift the ball so that it's bouncing when struck.
Exercise B23: Pass the ball to PB, who must shoot it first time.
Exercise B24: Toss the ball underhand to PB, who shoots it after the first bounce.
Exercise B25: PB tosses to you; you must hit a full volley. The toss from PB must be challenging and accurate.
Exercise B26: PB plays the ball to you; you must use a fake or feint before shooting.

Tips for doing this shooting and instep drive:
- Lock your foot [point the toe down] to form a firm striking surface.
- Keep your head down and focused on the ball.
- Hit through the ball. Follow through with your whole body for more power.
- Put your weight on your plant foot and snap your shooting leg into the shot.
- Don't be stiff or mechanical when shooting. Use your arms for balance.
- Place your plant foot next to or just slightly behind the ball.
- Before shooting, glance up to practice looking for where the goalkeeper is.
- Practice shooting curving balls and getting accuracy from the side of your foot as well as your instep.

OTHER SHOOTING EXERCISES USING A GOAL, WALL, OR KICKBOARD:

Exercise B27: Place a cone 3-5 yards away from you, dribble up to the cone, make a quick move past the cone, then shoot.

Exercise B28: Play 1 vs. 1 with your partner in the penalty area. You can also practice accuracy shooting by playing this game where the players cannot shoot using the instep drive. All shots must be from a curved ball using the inside of the foot or the outside of the foot.

Exercise B 29: Practice shooting off of a full dribble. Players aged 14 and up should shoot from 18 to 20 yards out; other players should shoot from 12 to 15 yards.

Exercise B30: PB stands in front of a hurdle or another safe obstacle that is 1-2 feet high. You stand two yards to the right or left of PB. PB passes the ball to you and leaps over the hurdle. You 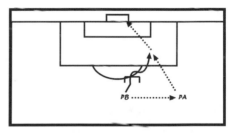 either: A) Play a pass on the ground for PB to shoot or B) Pick up the ball and bounce it underhand in the path of PB to shoot. This exercise helps PB with shooting a ball when he is a step off stride in his running onto the ball.

Exercise B31: Stand with your back to goal, 12 to 18 yards away-depending upon your age and shooting ability. PB, standing five yards behind you, tosses the ball over your shoulder; you must turn quickly and shoot. Put a one- or two-touch limit on this exercise. See Tips for Exercise 32

Exercise B32: Stand on the end line several yards wide of a goalpost and throw (underhand or sidearm) a bouncing ball to PB, who is standing in the penalty area about 12 to 15 yards from goal. The ball should bounce once before PB strikes it. Occasionally toss the ball to make PB stretch to get to it. This is good practice for shooting because players will get many chances at balls where they are off balance, have to stretch for the ball or have to strike a bouncing ball. Occasionally throw a ball to PB that shorthops right in front of him.

Players generally don't like to hit shots like this or to do these kinds of drills because they are very difficult. It is however an extremely valuable drill. Remember that the ball won't always roll exactly the way you want it to in a game.

Tip for doing this exercise:
To be able to put volleys, half volleys and bouncing balls on goal, you must dip the opposite shoulder, bend your body to get good contact on the ball, get your leg extended, and not lean back.

Exercise B33: First Time Shots
Goal: To be able to correctly shoot balls that run across your body.

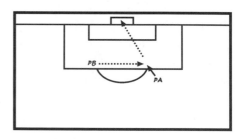

Part I
PB is standing 8 yards to your left. PB plays a pass that you must shoot with a first time shot. You may either A) let the ball run across your body and shoot or B) shoot the ball first before it runs across your body. You must shoot this ball with a first time shot. This is another difficult but valuable shot to learn.

Part II
PB is standing on the endline 2-3 yards to the side of the goalpost. You are directly in line with PB 12-18 yards from

goal. PB plays a ball back to you that you must shoot first time.

Tips for doing this exercise:
- Lean over the ball when striking it. Don't lean back
- Take just a little power off of this shot and make sure that it is accurate.
- Hitting first time shots are tough for goalkeepers to save because it is difficult for them to get their feet set and they don't often pick up the ball visually very well.

Exercise B34: Diagonal Runs
Goal: To develop the ability
to score from diagonal runs

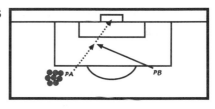

Set up 8-10 balls to one side of the penalty area, about 22 yards from goal. PB standing about 15 yards from goal makes a diagonal sprint across the penalty area. Play a ball wide enough so that PB can run onto it and get a shot on goal. PB should receive the pass about 8-10 yards from goal.

This is a difficult shot but players must practice it because it is a very useful play in the penalty area. Running diagonally across goal opens up a crowded penalty area and takes defenders out of good defending positions. Both the run and the pass require great timing.

Tips for doing this exercise:
- Practice making the runs and receiving passes from both sides of the box, using both feet to shoot.
- You must sprint across the box and you must be able to get your body turned so that you can get a shot on goal.

Exercise B35: Getting off quick shots
Goal: To be able to get off a quick shot without a long stride into the ball.

PB lines up 6-8 balls in a row about a foot apart. You shoot continuously without taking a long stride into the ball. This exercise is beneficial because many times the ball will be right on your foot and there is no time for a long back swing or run up to the ball. See Exercise B17.

Exercise B36: Control and volley
Goal: To be able to take balls out of the air and turn and volley.

PB tosses the ball to your chest or thigh. Take the ball off your chest or thigh and volley it on goal.

Exercise B37: Turn and shoot
Goal: To be able to play with your back to goal

Line up 8-10 soccer balls outside the penalty area. PB has his or her back to goal. Play a pass to PB, who has two touches to turn and get a shot on goal.
Keep the ball extremely close to you because you will lose it in a crowded penalty area. This is why exercise B35 is extremely valuable. Exercise B35 gives you the confidence to keep the ball in close and snap off a quick shot without a long stride into the ball.

TYPES OF TURNS TO PRACTICE:
- Inside of the foot.
- Outside of the foot.
- Cut the ball behind the planted leg.
- Use a body swerve or lunge before receiving the pass.
- Push or chop the ball across your body. Many turns in tight space require a little pass back (pushing the ball

back just a little at an angle, allowing you to turn your body and shoot). If done correctly it looks like you are passing the ball back to yourself in order to be able to turn the body to shoot.
- Step to the ball. Bringing the defender with you, let the ball run across your body, turn and shoot. This is an excellent move to use when a defender is overplaying you to one side. This move is excellent for freezing a defender, but can be difficult to pull off in a packed penalty area.
- Lift the ball slightly as you receive it, turn and shoot. Players should learn to get a feel for where the defender is by glancing around or by extending their arms back to find out where the defender is.

 Players can get a good turn on goal by drifting toward the far post as the play is building up on the flank and coming to the ball on an angle that allows them to receive the ball in a half-turned position.

Exercise B38: Near post goals
Goal: To be able to finish off crosses at the near post

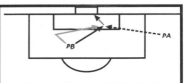

Line up 8-10 balls on the flank about 12 yards from the endline. Drive balls at head height or on the ground to the near post for PB to finish.

Tips for finishing at the near post:
- Start by hitting dead balls until some accuracy and the correct timing of the run from PB is established.
- You should run toward the far post before the cross arrives if there is enough time to do so. This allows the goal scorer to face the goal area when turning toward the player serving the ball. The shooter will have the maximum amount of goal at which to shoot once the ball is received. This also allows the goal scorer to be half turned toward the goal, improving the chance of scoring.

Usually there is more time to do this than players think. Make this run toward the far post before the flank player is running onto a ball or preparing to cross.

- Make a well-timed sprint into the space to get the near post goal.

- Hold off your run until your teammate is ready to cross the ball. Holding your run into the box increases your chances to get a good shot on goal and makes you more difficult to mark.

- The timing between the player who is crossing the ball and the goal scorer must be very precise

- If the defender tightens up on the attacker because of this run it often leaves a path to get inside of the defender to the near post

- Running toward the far post also helps you get on the blind side of the defender marking you. If that defender loses sight of you, you have the choice of running back toward the near post or waiting for a cross at the far post.

> *Cues that tell you when your teammate is ready to cross the ball:*
> - When he brings his leg back to cross.
> - When he lifts his head.
> - When he gets near the end line.

Note: Good goal scorers work hard to get into good positions. They shake a defender and sprint to open space in the penalty area. Anticipate the pass and keep your body in a position where you can take a quick shot or get a good chance for a header.

Exercise B39:The Far post Goal: Scoring goals from crosses to the far post.

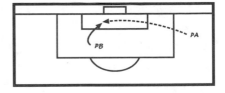

Cross balls to the far post and to mid-goal for PB to finish. PB must work on the timing of his runs and attacking high crosses and driven crosses.

Tips for doing this exercise:
- Get up and attack the cross.
- Keep your eyes open.
- Concentrate on making good contact with the ball.
- Attack the ball by thrusting your shoulders, neck, and head into the ball.
- Practice this exercise often under realistic conditions. The timing that you develop will help you score goals.
- Practice heading the ball down when it is appropriate.
- Remember that you don't have to be tall to score goals from headers

SCORING COMBINATIONS THAT SHOULD BE PRACTICED

A) The Early Diagonal Cross
This combination is effective because:

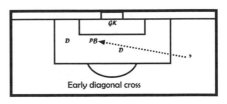

Early diagonal cross

1. The penalty area is wide open.
2. If the cross is put into the right spot, it makes it very difficult for the goalkeeper to judge as well as reach.
3. The defenders' bodies are not shaped up (turned) in a good position to clear away crosses. Defenders are usually turned the wrong way and are facing the goal they are defending. This makes it easier to get on the blind side of defenders.

B) Diagonal Balls Played Low Across the Box

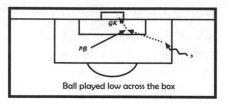
Ball played low across the box

Angle your dribble in toward the penalty area. Because of the reasons listed above (Section A) the diagonal ball is always a dangerous ball.

Also, this angled run makes it easier to cross the ball because the player's body is shaped up better to be accurate with the cross. The player doesn't have to cross the ball across his planted foot; his stride is very natural and fluid into the ball.

C. Balls Played Back from the Endline

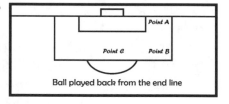
Ball played back from the end line

Any ball played back from the end line is more dangerous for the defense if it is played directly back (from point A to point B), because it has less chance of being intercepted (like a pass from point A to point C).

D. Crosses hit with the outside of the foot

If PA is a left-footed player, a low ball driven with the outside of the left foot can be very dangerous and deceptive. The same is true with a right-footed player coming down the left wing. If you are dribbling with the ball on the outside of your foot the cross is just a natural stride into the ball. The same is true with a right-footed player coming down the left wing. Because it is difficult to lift this ball, it will most likely be driven into the near post area instead of lofted to the far post.

DEFENDING EXERCISES FOR TWO PLAYERS
You can improve your defensive skills with almost any 1 v 1 competitive situation.

Exercise B40: 1 vs. 1 Defending
Goal: To improve the ability of 1 vs. 1 defending in all players.

Play 1 vs. 1 with PB in an area measuring 15 yards by 15 yards with two goals. Work on channeling, stance, containment, patience and holding onto the ball once you win it.

Tips for defenders in situations where the attacking player has turned and is facing the defender:
- Close players down. Cutting down a dribbler's space is the best way to limit his time and options. Allowing too much space lets a player lift his head and see the whole field.
- Many defenders give away too much space to the attacking player. However, if you are concerned about the attacker's speed, be careful not to get too close to him. It is always better to concede a little ground than to be beaten.
- Channel the attacking player where you want him to go, in most cases to the side of his weaker foot, by getting close to him. Too many defenders give away too much space.
- Take up a stance at a 45-degree angle instead of a right angle. This way the opponent cannot get you going one way and then play the ball across your body. Make him turn and step across his own body.
- Defenders should work on their footwork. Stay on the balls of your feet. Defenders should stay low and really work on their change of direction and footwork.
- Use restraint. Don't sprint out of control at a player with the ball. When a defender is off balance, he is easier to beat on the dribble. Be patient, and force the dribbler to beat you.

- Know your tackling range (don't lunge for a ball that you can't get) and tackling abilities. A misjudged tackle can have devastating results. Some defenders try to wind up and be too forceful in the tackle. It is better to take shorter jabs at the ball and break up the play than to miss the tackle.
- Know when to use the slide tackle-only when you are clearly beaten or have no other choice. It's best, though, to stay on your feet. The slide tackle can be a very effective defensive move. However, it should be used only in situations where the defender cannot win the ball by tackling in a standing position.
- Recognize your speed as you close down space. Approaching an attacker who is in control too quickly can leave you off balance and create big problems. When approaching a tackle, look at the ball and not the attacker's feet or hips.
- When approaching a tackle, don't get caught watching the opponent's fakes or feints with the ball. Watch the ball instead. Also, through experience, you will learn to pick up on certain cues and moves that will give away where the attacking player wants to go.
- Attackers will often try to push the ball past a defender and beat him to the ball with speed. Increased exposure to this situation will help the defender learn to anticipate this move. Recover to the ball goal-side of the attacker, so that your body is always between the ball and the goal
- Stay alert after the opponent has passed the ball. Your job is not done yet.
- Defenders must play hard, and it is not always fun. Playing good defense pays off when you win the ball and restart the attack.
- Develop moves that enable you to hold the ball and relieve pressure once you win the ball back. See Section "Moves to Relieve Pressure"

Exercise B41: Heading
Goal: To develop heading skill
(both attacking and defending)

PART I
Toss the ball to PB, who jumps to attack the ball at the highest point possible and head it back to you. The ball should be thrown with a significant arc so that PB can rise to meet it as it descends. This helps with clearing crosses from the penalty areas and winning the ball on punts and clearances.

PART II
Cross the ball to PB, who jumps to head the ball at goal.

Tips for attacking heading:
- Timing is everything. Jumping at just the right moment is crucial. This skill takes many hours of practice to develop
- Keep your eyes open and watch the ball.
- Use your arms to get elevation.
- Make good clean contact with the ball.
- Head the ball down when appropriate. Practice this under realistic conditions.
- Practice single and double leg takeoffs.
- In all heading situations it is important to get to the ball first. Also, every player will have a different heading strategy based on his physical attributes.
- Many goals are scored in today's game by players getting into the near post. Most of these players have quick, explosive upward movements to get to the ball before their opponent.
- Practice the timing required to score at the near post. Shape your body correctly to maximize your chances at getting a strike at goal. Don't fear running into the near post.

- Practice sprinting into the near post. This is the best way to lose defenders and to master the timing needed to score goals at the near post.

Tips for Defensive Heading
- Get to the ball first
- Practice getting elevation by using your arms to thrust you upward.
- Head the ball high, wide, and far.
- Shape up your body (turn it) in such a way that gives you the best chance of winning the ball. This position would be facing your own goal or half -turned toward your own goal.
- Always challenge for the header even if you don't think you can win it cleanly
- Don't lean into the attacker or put your arms on his back. Refs love to call this one!
- On a low driven cross don't stand behind the attacker, step in front of him to win the ball

Exercise B42: Dribbling and shielding skills

Utilize exercises that involve players playing 1 vs. 1 will provide an environment for developing dribbling and shielding skills. (See exercises B40, C9 and C16).

Tips for doing this exercise:
- To be able to shield the ball, wedge your body between the defender and the ball and keep a lower center of gravity.
- You don't have to be bigger than the defender to shield the ball from them. You do however need to be quicker and smarter.
- Develop your own collection of moves that will enable you to be able to shield the ball.

EXERCISES FOR THREE PLAYERS

NOTE: The exercise description makes reference to the word **you**. You are player A in this section

Exercise C1: Passing Triangle
Goal: To improve passing and ball control

Three players stand 12-15 yards apart in a triangle. Pass the ball around using the inside of the foot, the outside of the foot, and the instep. Pass the ball around in a triangle as many times as possible in a one-minute time period using the following conditions:
- One-touch
- Two-touch
- 3-4 touches with fast feet.
- Touches with the weaker foot-i.e., left foot for righties, etc.

Tips for doing this exercise:
- Hips, legs, and feet need to be quick and lively.
- Always turn your hips and shape your body so that you can pass in at least two different directions.
- The first touch should set up your second touch. It is important to balance and readjust your feet after the first touch on the ball in order to make a clean second touch. Do not limit options with the first touch or you will be forced to play the ball to a specific side.
- Practice passing with the outside of the foot when that type of pass is a faster play.
- Practice the instep chop pass.

Exercise C2: Turning
Goal: To improve passing, controlling, and turning with the ball

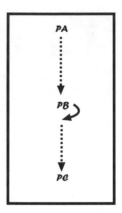

Three players stand in a straight line about 6-8 yards apart from each other. Play a pass to PB, who should turn and play a pass to PC in just two touches. Repeat the exercise 10 times or for one minute.

Tips for doing this exercise:
Practice all types of turns:
- Inside of the foot
- Outside of the foot
- Cutting the ball behind the standing leg
- Chopping the ball across the body with either the inside or outside of the foot

- When there is no defender present adjust your body in a position where you are half-turned as you receive the ball on the first touch. This can only be done if there is no defender on you.
- Practice turning with the first touch and then passing with the outside of the foot with the second touch.
- Players are often coached to take a look over their shoulders before the ball is played toward them. In tight spaces, you need to look around well before the pass is played to you or you need to use your arms and hands to feel for defenders.
- You also should rely on information from the player who passes the ball, such as "man on" or "turn left." Communication is a vital part of good combination play and cannot be overstressed. Practice verbal interaction as you practice other skills.

Exercise C3: Quick Feet
Goal: To develop quick feet and a quick mind

Players form a line similar to that in Exercise C2. Play the ball to PB and as you do, call out "1" or "2." The number indicates how many touches PB can use get the ball to PC. On a pass where you call "1" touch, PB should practice the in-step chop pass instead of relying on flick or heel passes. You must give the information immediately after making the pass.

Exercise C4: Long Chipped Balls (Advanced)
Goal: Developing the ability to play long balls quickly

Start in a straight line, with players at least 20 yards apart. Play a chip to PB, who must turn and play a chip to PC.

Tips for doing this exercise:
- Try to complete the exercise with just two touches. If the ball is not controlled down to the ground on the first touch, then PB should take an additional touch to bring the ball under control. Do not hit the ball if it is bouncing around.
- Use different techniques to control the ball and learn which one leaves you in the best position to deliver a well-hit chip. Also practice hitting chipped balls with the outside of the foot.
- Practice chipping the ball without taking a long stride into the ball. If PB finds that he has controlled the ball too close to the body, he should practice hitting the ball with out taking this long stride. This will help players when they compete at a faster pace. (See Exercise B17.)

Exercise C5: Playing Long Balls
Goal: Developing accuracy on long passes

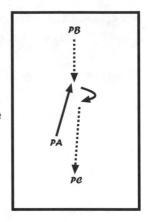

The three players should be spaced 20-25 yards apart; with you (Player A) in the center.
Check (move) to PB and turn after controlling a short pass from PB.
After turning with the ball you must lift your head and play a long ball to PC.
You then check (move) to PC and repeat the exercise by controlling, turning and playing a long ball back to PB.

Try to send the ball by using one touch to turn and one touch to pass. Players also should practice this pass with the weaker foot and with the outside of the foot.

Exercise C6: Outside of the foot passing
Goal: To develop the ability to play the ball with outside of the foot from a full speed dribble.

Use the same setup as in the exercise above. In this exercise, you receive a short pass from PB, then turn and speed dribble to PC using only the outside of the foot. Play a pass to PC from at least 15 yards away with the outside of the foot without breaking stride. You now repeat the exercise after checking to receive a pass from PC.

Exercise C7: Clearing Headballs
Goal: To develop defensive heading skills

You and PB and PC line up about 10 yards apart with PB in the center.
Toss the ball underhand to PB, who jumps to maximum height to head the ball back to you.
Repeat the process with PC tossing underhand to PB 25 times, or for one minute.

Tips for doing this exercise:
- Practice one and two-leg takeoffs.
- Attack the ball by throwing your shoulders back, getting your arms up and thrusting your torso into the ball.
- Practice the timing of your heading. The correct timing on headballs is essential.

PART II
You are on the flank with about 10 balls. PB and PC are in the penalty area. Play balls into the penalty area for PB or PC to clear.

In the next phase PB is the defender and PC is the attacker. Cross balls to the near and far post. The two players compete to win the ball.

Exercise C8: Skill Builder
Goal: To develop overall ball skill

You and PB are about 15 yards apart, with PC in the middle. Both you and PB have a ball in your hand. Underhand toss the ball to PB (chest or thigh) who must two touch the ball back to you. PB turns and repeats the process with PC.

Next the players form lines in the same set up as the exercise above. Using several balls, you and PB randomly serve underhand tosses in the air and passes on the ground to PC, who must one- or two-touch the ball back to the player who served it. Do this exercise for 1 minute.

Various skills can be practiced when you and PB randomly alternate serves to PC. For example, you can toss underhand passes for PC to head and PB can pass balls on the ground for PC to two-touch back.

Other skills to practice:
- Headballs
- Passing the ball on the ground so PC has two touches to return the ball to the server.
- Tossing the ball underhand to PC, who has two touches to get it back to the server.
- Tossing the ball underhand to PC, who volleys it back to the server.
- While serving the ball to PC, call out a number, which indicates the number of touches PC has to return the pass.

Exercise C9: 1 vs. 1
Part I
Goal: To improve dribbling skills.

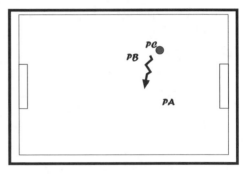

In an area about 15-20 yards wide, 15-20 yards long and playing with two goals, have all three players play "every man for himself". This will create a 1 vs 2 situation all over the field and is great for developing dribbling skills. Players can score at any goal that they wish.

Part II
Using the same field dimensions (15- 20 yards wide, 15-20 yards long) square with two goals, play 1 vs. 1 against PB. PC should be on the side with a constant supply of balls ready to be served into the game. PC should pass the

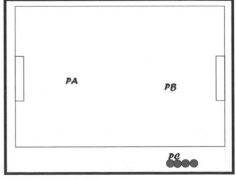

ball into play to the appropriate player. No free first touches are allowed. Players can score at either goal or you may set up a situation where each player is assigned a goal to defend. Younger players can play with 3 or 4 goals if they choose to. Play against PB until one of the players scores two goals. PC will play the winner. The loser serves the balls.

Part III

All three players now play to a full size goal inside of the penalty area. Play 1 vs. 1 against PB, with PC serving as the goalkeeper. After winning back the ball, each player takes the ball

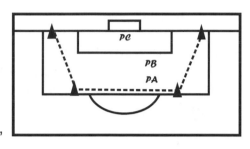

back behind the restraining lines. This creates a situation similar to 1 vs. 1 basketball. Compete with PB until two goals are scored; the winner then plays PC. You may also play 1 vs. 2 inside of the penalty area.

Tips for doing this exercise:
- Develop your own repertoire of moves that will allow you to hold onto the ball and get shots off.

Exercise C10: Turn and Shoot
Goal: To improve players' ability to play with their backs to goal.

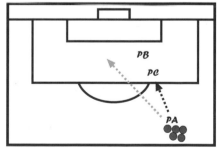

PB is marking PC, who has his back to goal inside the penalty area. You serve in passes. PC must try to turn and hit shots on goal. PC should get the first touch to be free.

Tips for doing this exercise:
Learn how to create space so you can shoot. To do so PC must consider the following:

- Make a diagonal run across the penalty area. Your pass must be played wide enough so that PC can turn his body to hit the shot. (see exercise B34)
- PC checks (moves) back to PB to create some space. Try extending your arm to seal off the defender.
- PC tries to get behind the defense if PB marks too closely by making something similar to a back-door cut in basket ball.
- Another way to get behind the defense through combination play: When the ball is played in to PC, if PB is marking too closely, PC should play a wall pass combination to get behind you.

Players should always try to get behind the defense whenever possible.

TIPS FOR ATTACKING PLAYERS WHEN TRYING TO GET BEHIND THE DEFENSE: ADVANCED

- Curve your run so that when you receive a pass you are facing the goal. Curving a run also allows for a greater margin of error for the player who is making the pass.
- Whenever the player who is receiving the pass is equal (meaning, next to) the defender, he should make his first touch towards goal to eliminate the defender with a quick burst of speed on the dribble. Too many attacking players stop the ball and allow the defender to get back into the game.

Shooting Exercises
Also please review all the shooting exercises listed for two players. Exercises B18-39

Exercise C11: Shooting balls coming back to you
Goal: To improve first-time shooting ability

You and PC stand 18-20 yards apart, with both players playing goalkeeper defending a goal that is behind you. PB is located halfway between you and PC. PB plays a pass to you; you either first-time shoot or take two touches to shoot.

Exercise C12: Breakaways
Goal: To improve scoring on breakaways

Stand 25-30 yards away from PB, each of you defending a goal. PC stands behind you in the goal ready to take your place in the next round. Begin dribbling; you have 5 seconds to score on PB. As soon as the play is completed PB tries to score on PC within the five second time allotment. Repeat the exercise with PC trying to score on you.

Exercise C12a: Breakaways II
Goal: To improve scoring ability on breakaways

Standing next to PB (25 yards away from goal) play a pass to PB, who has 5 seconds to score a goal with PC playing goalkeeper. Then all players should switch roles.

Exercise C13: Crossing Balls I Advanced
Goal: To be able to cross a ball under pressure

Play against PB, 1 vs.1, on the flank in a space 30 yards long by 12-15 yards wide. (From the edge of the penalty area to the sideline. See diagram) Try to beat PB and then send in a cross into the penalty area to PC. If PB wins the ball, he tries to get a cross into the penalty area. Have several balls lined up outside of the playing area. As soon as the ball goes out of play, the first player to retrieve a ball can restart the exercise. If playing with just two players, place cones or markers in the penalty area to serve as targets for the cross.

Exercise C14: Crossing Balls II Advanced
Goal: To develop the ability to cross the ball under pressure

Set up as shown in the diagram. Push a pass to PB. PB runs onto the ball at full speed and crosses it into the penalty area for PC to finish.

As a variation, push a pass to PB, who is being chased by PC starting from about 5 yards behind. Set markers in the penalty area indicating key spots where the ball should be served. You may also do this exercise with PB starting out dribbling and being chased by PC. You may stand in the penalty area trying to finish off crosses from PB.

As another variation of this exercise have PC run next to PB as if to shadow him. PC should not intercept the cross but should apply enough pressure so that PB feels the presence of a player in that position.

Tips for doing this exercise: **ADVANCED**
- When running onto a ball at top speed, come around the outside of the ball and make solid contact. Don't try to hit the ball too hard. It already has forward speed on it, so a solid contact will be sufficient.
- When running onto a ball that you are going to cross, lift your head up and take a glance in the penalty box to see the position of the goalkeeper and your teammates.
- Listen for calls from your teammates. When you are under intense pressure, this will help you decide where to cross the ball.
- Don't try to be perfect. Get the ball into the penalty area in a place where the goalkeeper cannot get to it. The biggest waste is a cross that goes out of bounds or right to the goalkeeper.
- Whenever possible, angle your run or dribble in from the flank towards goal. This will shape your body in a better position to cross the ball.

Exercise C15: Crossing Balls III
Goal: To develop the ability to cross from the opposite side of the field.

Coming from the left flank, angle your dribble in and cross the ball, using the outside of your foot, to PB and PC. This type of cross should be driven because it is difficult to float in a cross with the outside of the foot.

Exercise C16:Defending for Three Players
Goal: To improve the ability of all players to mark up and defend.

The ideal situation for practicing defending with three players is to utilize the following set up:
You serve as the neutral player who feeds passes into the attacking player. You have 10 balls lined up about 15 yards outside of the playing grid. PC is closely marking PB inside of that playing grid. PB and PC play 1 vs.1 (with 2 goals) in an area about 20 yards wide and 20 yards long.
You send passes in from 15 yards away. This will give the defending player the opportunity to defend against long passes and the opportunity to clear the incoming balls away. Vary the incoming balls between passes in the air and passes on the ground. The play will continue until PC wins the ball or plays it outside of the grid. When this happens, immediately send another pass to PB to keep concentration levels high and to keep a steady flow going. After 10 turns as a defender PC switches roles with PB.

Defending Situations That Will Come Up
- Defending when the attacking player has turned and faced the defender. (See Exercise B40)
- Marking the attacking player with his back to goal.
- Marking the player who has taken up a wide position on the field.

Tips for doing this exercise:
When a defender is placed in situations where: A) you are marking a player from behind or B) you are marking a player who has taken a wide position keep the following points in mind:
- Don't let the player you are marking receive a pass in a space behind you.

- Don't ball-watch. Don't watch the ball as your opponent is getting in behind you.
- Don't play too close to your attacker so that he can get in behind you because you have over-committed.
- Play the proper distance away from the player you are marking. Remember:
- The farther the ball is away from the player you are marking, the farther you can back away and play off of him.
- Ask yourself: if the ball is played to this player, can I win the ball or intercept the pass? Or can I at least get to the player and close him down by the time the ball gets to him? If the answers are yes, then the playing distance from the player is correct.
- If there is pressure from your teammate on the player in possession, if you are quick to step in front of an attacker and intercept a pass, you can mark your opponent shoulder to shoulder instead of marking from behind.
- Pay attention! A smart attacker will try to: (a) draw you out of good defending position, (b) lull you to sleep and then check back quickly for the ball and receive it in a dangerous position, (c) draw you away and then get into a position where he can use his body as a shield between you and the ball, (d) get on your blind side, especially in the penalty area. You will either lose that player or that player might get you to adjust your defensive position in order to get an inside path to the goal.
- These are your priorities, in order, when the ball is played to a player you are marking: (a) step in and win the ball, (2) don't let the attacking player turn, (3) tackle the ball as the player turns with it, (4) at the very least, be in control when the player turns on you and faces goal.
- When an attacking player turns and faces goal, you start to apply the principles explained in 1 vs. 1 defending when an attacker is facing the defender.
- If there is pressure from your teammate on the player in possession, if you are quick to step in front of an attacker and intercept a pass, you can mark your opponent shoulder to shoulder instead of marking from behind.

Fun Practice Games

SOCCER CROQUET. Set up a series of cones and have players advance by passing through these cones as if they were croquet wickets. Players are allowed to hit another players' ball just as in croquet.

HORSE. Play this game just like the popular basketball shooting game. The first player must successfully call and complete a shot, chip, dribbling move, or a combination of the above skills. The other players must complete the same skill or be charged with a letter.

ALL GAMES INVOLVING 1 VS.1 (see C9, C16,B40)

GAMES INVOLVING A KICKBOARD OR WALL (see B8 and B9, Soccer Squash and Soccer Tennis)

VOLLEY CONES. Using a pair of large traffic cones, place the ball on top of a cone and have players volley the ball off of the cone.

FOUR-GOAL SOCCER. Two or more players compete in an area that would be an appropriate size for the number of players involved (for four or more players: 20 x 20 yards; for 1 vs.1: 10 x 10 yards). Set up four goals. The players can score at any of the four goals. Having four goals present enables the players to change direction quickly as well as score lots of goals. This game can also be played with two goals designated to one team and two goals designated to another team.

SIX- OR EIGHT-GOAL SOCCER. Use the same setup described above, except six or eight goals are now used.

MEGA GOALS. Numerous goals are set up around the field. Players have one minute to dribble in and out of as many goals as they can, and compete for the highest number of goals scored in one minute.

SOCCER GOLF. The players involved try to pass to one of the targets that have been designated as a "hole." Each time the player takes a kick, it counts as a stroke-just as in golf. Advanced players can make the game more challenging by hitting the ball with the left foot, the outside of the foot, striking a moving ball off the dribble, or receiving a pass before trying to hit one of the targets.

SLALOM DRIBBLING. Set up a series of cones that are staggered like a ski slalom. Players dribble in and out of these cones as quickly as possible. The players can time themselves to see which players make it through the course the fastest.

SHOOTER AND KEEPER. (see B18-26)

HEADING PENDULUM. Place a slightly deflated ball attached to a safe anchor similar to a tetherball. Players can practice heading the ball without constantly chasing it.

SOCCER CRABS. In a small area, allow one player to dribble while the other players defend in a crab position (seated, using the hands and feet to move). Set up goals and put time limitations on the defenders. This exercise will provide good dribbling practice and lots of fun.

SOCCER BASEBALL. Set up bases. One player rolls or kicks the ball to a second player. The second player kicks it and tries to touch as many bases as possible until the other players can score a goal. To score a goal, the other players in the field must get the ball and pass it through a goal made up of cones located around home plate.

SOCCER SNIPER. Place a series of cones down in any formation you wish. Players must knock down as many cones as possible with a shot or a pass.

TIRE SHOOT. Hang a tire from a tree and practice chipping or shooting shots through or off of the tire.

RELAY RACES. Use a soccer ball, and let your imagination take over!

Fitness

RUNNING PROGRAM

- Before beginning this running program become familiar with the terms that are used.
- Wear comfortable running shoes that fit correctly to avoid injuries.
- Do a good 10 minute stretch before doing any running.

Terms you should be familiar with:

Steady run - faster than a jog but not a sprint. You should be able to maintain the same pace for at least 25-30 minutes. The times of your steady run should increase each week.

60% run - a run that you can sustain an even pace for 90 seconds

75% sprint - a run that you can sustain an even pace for 45-50 seconds (weeks 1-4) and 50-60 seconds (weeks 5-8) and 65-70 seconds (weeks 9-end of program)

90% sprint - a run that you can sustain an even pace for 30 seconds (weeks 1-4) and 35 seconds (weeks 5-8)

Sprint Hard with maximum effort - 100% sprint

Recovery run - Slow jog

- If at any time the program is too easy just increase the pace and intensity

WEEK 1

Day 1 - Run at a steady pace for 20 minutes.

Day 2 - Run at a 75% sprint pace for 45-50 seconds
Rest/walk for 3 minutes in between. Do six sets of this.

Day 3 - Do six 100 yards sprints in 16-18 seconds. (Rest
for 40 seconds then repeat) Do this for 2 sets of 8. Rest 3
minutes between sets. Times should be faster during the
2nd set.

Strength training - 3 per week (see workout sheet at the
end of this chapter)

Plyometrics (Twice per week) - #1 Skipping rope
#2 Jump and stick.

Play 1-2 games per week.
Practice with the ball everyday.

WEEK 2

Day 1 -   Run steady for 25 minutes. The time should be
faster than last week.

Day 2 - Run 90% sprint for 30 seconds, jog for 30 seconds,
do 10 sets of this. After completing this, run steady for 2
minutes and then walk fast for two minutes. Finish with a
ten minute steady run.

Strength Training - 2-3 per week

Plyometrics - #1 Skipping rope
#2 Jump and stick.

Play 1-2 games per week.
Practice with the ball everyday.

WEEK 3

Day 1 - Sprint hard with maximum effort for ten seconds then slow down and jog for 20 seconds. Do two sets, 5 minutes for each set (10 minutes total). Finish with a 10 minute steady run.

Day 2 - Fartlek (speed play) run for 30 minutes:

To simulate the demands of the game with quick starts and stops.

Run continuously in the following order: sprints, steady runs, and then jog.

This program has three phases:
1) Sprints (10-15 seconds)
2) Steady run (harder than a jog) for 30 seconds- 1 minute
3) Recovery Run (30 seconds)

Day 3 - Steady run for 30 minutes. The time should be faster than last week.

Strength - 3 twice per week

Plyometrics - (Twice per week) #1 Skip rope
                                    #2 Jump and stick.

Play 1-2 games per week.
Practice with ball every day.

WEEK 4

Day 1- Sprint 100 yards at 16-18 seconds. 30 seconds rest between sprints. Do 4 sprints per set. Do 3 sets (12 sprints total) of this with 3 minute rest between sets.

Finish with a 10 minute steady cool-down run.
Day 2 - (60%) run for 90 seconds with 3 minute rest between sets. Do (8) 90 second runs.

Day 3 - 30 minute steady run. The time should be faster than last week.

Strength Training - 3 times per week.
Plyometrics - #1 Skipping rope
　　　　　　　#2 Jump ups and squat jumps.

Play 1-2 games per week.
Practice everyday with the ball.

WEEK 5

Day 1 - 45 second run (75%), 30 second jog recovery, do 10 sets.

Day 2 - 1 minute run (75%) with 30 second recovery. Do 5 sets.

Day 3 - 30 minutes steady run. The time should be faster than last week.

Strength and Plyometrics - Same as week 4

Play 1-2 games per week.
Practice with ball every day.

WEEK 6

Day 1 - 100% sprint for 10 seconds. Jog for 10-15 seconds. Do 2 sets of 6 minutes. Do a 3 minute walk between sets.

Day 2 - See week 2, Day 2

Strength - 3 times per week

Plyometrics - # 1 Skipping rope
　　　　　　　# 4 Lunges
Play 1-2 games per week.
Practice with ball everyday.

WEEK 7

Day 1 - (7) 100 yard sprints 16-18 seconds with 30 seconds rest between runs. 2 sets (14 sprints total), 3 minute rest between sets.

Finish with a 10 minute steady cool down run.

Day 2 - (8) 90 second runs (75%) with 3 minutes recovery (slow jog) between run.

Day 3 - 30 minute steady run. The time should be faster than last week.

Strength and Plyometrics - Same as week 6

Play 1-2 games per week.
Practice with ball everyday.

WEEK 8

Light running or no running at all

Strength training - 3 per week

Plyometrics - (Twice per week) #1 Skipping rope
                                    # 5 Zig Zag Bounds

Play 1-2 games per week

WEEK 9

Day 1 - 30 second (90%) sprint, 30 second jog between as a recovery. Do 12 reps.

Day 2 - 1 minute (75%) run with 2 minute recovery between runs. Do 6 sets.

Day 3 - 30 minute steady run. The time should be faster than week 7.

No strength or plyometrics training

Practice with ball everyday

Limit the number of games played per week if practice begins within 2 weeks.

WEEK 10

Day 1 -   30 second (90%) sprint with 25 second jog as a recovery. Do 12 reps. 10 minute steady cool down run.

Day 2 - 30 minute steady run with 20 hard sprints (15-25 seconds) dispersed throughout.

Day 3 - 30 minute steady run. The time should be faster than last week.

Strength - 3 per week.

Plyometrics (Twice per week) #1 jump rope
                                    #6 180 jumps

Practice with ball everyday.
Limit the amount of games played each week if practice begins within 2 weeks.

Weeks 11 and 12 (if necessary). Follow the schedule for weeks 9 and 10 but increase the intensity of the workout.

FITNESS STANDARDS

Use the following standards to check your fitness level (Pick only one test to do at a time):

A) The 12 minute run.
After running for 12 minutes if you cover 1.5 miles that is considered fair condition for a soccer player.
1.75 miles is considered good condition for a soccer player.
2 miles is considered very good condition for a soccer player.
More than 2 miles is considered excellent for a soccer player.

B) Set the cones 40 yards apart. Run sprints up to the cone and back three times (240 yards total). Do this exercise in 45-50 seconds total. Repeat this exercise 4-6 times, maintaining consistent times with 45 seconds rest between.
Do six 60 yard sprints in 18 seconds maintaining consistent times with 40-50 seconds rest between sets.
Do ten 40 yard sprints in 8-10 seconds maintaining consistent times with 25-35 seconds rest in between sets.

Do all three runs in section B. If you can maintain consistent times in all three runs, you are in very good condition for soccer.

PLYOMETRICS

#1 Skipping Rope - do 10 sets of 50 skips of rope on first training day of the week.

#2 Jump and Stick - standing still, jump as far forward as possible off of 2 feet hold that postition for 5 seconds. Do this 5 times. Do 3 sets. Do this on second plyometrics training day.

#3 Jump Ups/Squat Jumps - Bend knees down in a squat then jump up as high as possible. Do 20 jumps. Do 3 sets on the first training day of the week.

#4 Lunges - standing still lunge forward as far as possible with the left leg. Move back to the starting position then lunge forward onto the right leg. Do 20 reps (10 with each leg) in 20 seconds. Do two sets.

#5 Zig Zag Bounds - set 10 cones or markers in a row. Alternate jumping over cones while moving forward diagonally (do 10 jumps). Do 2 sets of 10 jumps on the right foot. 2 sets of 10 jumps on the left foot. 2 sets of jumps on both feet. 6 sets total.

#6 180 Jumps - jump in place turning 180 degrees in the air, take-off immediately while turning in the opposite direction. 2 sets of 10 jumps. Do this on second plyometrics day of week.

Do not do these plyometrics exercises on back to back days.

It takes 8-12 weeks to get fit. If you wait until July or August to get fit, your play will suffer in the long run. The key to soccer fitness is to get in shape and STAY in shape. Use preseason as a way to get sharp not fit. Keep in mind that there is a difference between running fitness and real soccer fitness. Your first priority in the summer is to play games and practice with the ball. A close second priority is to follow the running schedule enclosed. It is also important to do plyometrics and weight training. However, if you do not weight train, you must do strength training by doing the alternate strength training schedule.

The running program utilizes sprints combined with some long steady runs. Follow the program and it will improve your fitness immensely. Start this program 10-12 weeks before the first week of practice.

STRENGTH TRAINING WORKOUT SHEET

To increase strength and power it is important to weight train three times per week for 8-12 weeks before preseason begins. The program listed below should take between 35-45 minutes. It is designed for soccer players who have busy schedules. Beginning weight trainers should do between 15-18 sets and should work up to 18-20 total. More advanced weight trainers can lift between 20-24 sets.

Make sure that you do a good warm-up stretch before lifting.

Use a weight that you can lift between 8-12 times for the upper body and 12-15 times for the lower body before you increase the weight of the bar or dumbell.

Important Factors to Consider.
1.)   Breathe in and out while lifting
2.)   Push out the last two repetitions even if you need a spotter to help you. The last two repetitions are when you gain strength.
3.)   Don't get caught up with how much weight you are lifting. Using the correct technique is most important.
4)   Emphasize speed in lifting. This will increase your overall quickness.

Day 1

Lat pull down	3-4 sets	
Low row	3 sets	BACK
- -		
Squats	3 sets	
Calf raises	3 sets	
Lunges	3 sets	LEGS
- -		
Dumbbell press	3-4 sets	
Upright row	3-4 sets	SHOULDERS

Day 2

Bench press	3 sets	
Dumbbell Fly on Bench	3-4 sets	CHEST

- -

Bent over fly with dumbbells	3 sets	
Lateral raises with dumbbells	3-4 sets	SHOULDERS

- -

Biceps curl	4-5 sets	
Triceps extension	4-5 sets	ARMS

Day 3

Bench press	3-4 sets	
Dumbbell flies on bench	3 sets	CHEST

- -

Lunges	2 sets	
Squats	2 sets	
Calf raises	2 sets	
Leg extensions	2 sets	
Leg curl	2 sets	LEGS

- -

Lat pull down	3 sets	
Low rows	3-4 sets	BACK

ABDOMINAL STRENGTH PROGRAM

A) **Curl Ups**- place hands across the chest, lower back flat on the ground, come up 12-18 inches off of the ground and return

B) **Twisting Sit Ups** - place hands behind the neck. Take left elbow and twist as you come up. Touch left elbow to the outside of the right knee. Do the same for the right side.

C) **Crunch** - same starting position. Bring feet up off of the ground and cross them. Elbows should be about 18 inches away from the knees. Sit up to bring elbows up to the knees.

D)   **Flutter Kicks** - Place hands under buttocks, keep
        knee straight, flutter kick legs while keeping them 6
        inches off the ground.

Do 200 repetitions using a combination of the exercises
above. Try to work up to a point where you can do 200
reps without breaking. Breathe consistently during the workout.

ALTERNATIVE PROGRAM FOR ABDOMINALS

Take a **medicine ball** that is of a weight which will
challenge you.

A)   Use a chopping motion to bring the medicine ball
        down to the knee - alternate chopping down to the
        right and left knees. Do 50 -75 times. Do two sets

B)   Use the same chopping motion and bring the medi-
        cine ball down to the ankles. Again alternate
        between chopping down to the right and left ankles.
        Do 50 - 75 times. Do two sets.

C)   Hold medicine ball out straight turn half way around
        to the right. Bring the ball back to the center and
        repeat the exercise going to the left- Do 50-75
        times. Do two sets.

WEIGHT TRAINING TERMS

Lat Pull Down (Gym Equipment)
- Grab bar with palms out (wider than shoulder)
- Sit on floor
- Pull bar down to chest under control
- Raise bar up until arms are fully extended

Low Row (Gym Equipment)
- From a seated position grab bar with palms out extended
  at the elbows   .
- Bend trunk and knees slightly. Lean torso back slightly
- Pull back to chest area. Bring the torso forward during this
  motion.
- Return to starting position

Squats
- Use squat racks and spotters
- Grab bar with palms up
- Place center of the bat on the upper back resting on
  shoulders
- Straighten legs to lift the barbell off the neck and step
  backward
- Under control, bend hips backward, bend knees and
  ankles
- Descend slowly until tops of thighs are parallel to floor
- Return to upright position under control

Overhead Dumbell Press
- From a standing or seated position take a dumbbell in
  each hand and hold them at shoulder height.
- Bring the dumbbells overhead while extending at the
  elbow.
- Bring the dumbbells together.
- Return to starting position.

Upright Row
- From a standing position, grab bar six to eight inches wide with palms down resting on thighs.
- Pull bar up to chin with elbows out.
- Return to starting position.

Bench Press
- Lie on bench with back flat and feet on ground.
- Grab bar with a wide grip, palms facing up.
- Bring bar down to chest.
- Return to strength position- be sure to keep lower back and feet on the floor.

Calf Raises
- Place the weight on top of the shoulders.
- Step on to the footplate (if available), placing the balls of the feet near the edge.
- Raise heels as high as possible.
- Return to starting position.

Lunges
- Place barbell on shoulders or hold dumbbells in each hand.
- Take a step forward with lead leg keeping the knee and toe in a straight alignment.
- Plant foot on floor and bend at the knee.
- Return to starting position.
- Repeat with opposite leg.

Leg Curl
- Lay face down on leg curl machine.
- Place ankles under the roller pad and place kneecap just over the edge of the pad.
- Pull lower legs toward buttocks.
- Return to starting position.

Lateral Raises with Dumbbells
- The body should be bent over at the hip so the upper body is parallel to the ground.
- Arms should be out straight.
- Using a light weight have dumbbells down touching each other above the knees in line with the chest.
- Raise arms up so that they become parallel to the ground.
- Return to the starting position.

Dumbbell Press On Bench
- Lie On Bench with back flat and feet on floor.
- Hold dumbbells at chest level - elbows bent.
- Bring dumbbells together as you extend at the elbows.
- Return to starting position.

Lateral Raises
- Hold dumbbells at side, arms straight, palms facing in.
- Bend at hip so that the trunk is parallel to the ground.
- Push to the dumbbells under control in an arc to shoulder level.
- Return to starting position.

Triceps Extension
- Take an easy curl bar and grip it 12-18 inches apart. Hold the bar behind the head with the elbows facing out.
- Extend the arms upward so that the elbows are completely locked out.
- Return to starting position.

ALTERNATE STRENGTH PROGRAM

If you have never participated in a weight training program you should work on the alternate strength program for 4-6 weeks before embarking on the weight training program listed here.

Do 4-6 sets of push ups- Do as many as you can using the correct (keeping body straight) technique- Rest 1-2 minutes between sets. Increase the repetitions and number of sets as you get stronger.

Do 3 sets of pull-ups.

Also Available from Reedswain

#185 **Conditioning for Soccer** ————————
by Raymond Verheijen
$19.95

#188 **300 Innovative Soccer Drills** ————————————
by Roger Wilkinson and Mick Critchell
$14.95

#290 **Practice Plans for Effective
Training** ————————————————
by Ken Sherry
$14.95

#787 **Attacking Schemes and
Training Exercises** ————————————
by Eugenio Fascetti and Romedio Scaia
$14.95

#788 **Zone Play** ————————————————
by Angelo Pereni and Michele di Cesare
$14.95

#792 **120 Competitive Games and
Exercises** ————————————————
by Nicola Pica
$14.95

#793 **Coaching the 5-3-2** ————————
by Eugenio Fascetti and Romedio Scaia
$14.95

www.reedswain.com or 800-331-5191

Also Available from Reedswain